KLAIRI LYKIARDOPOULOU

individuality
unity
MONAD

MEGAS SEIRIOS
Publications

ISBN: 978-960-7350-47-3

This book is published by **Megas Seirios Publications**, founded by the **Servers' Society Spiritual Centre** based in Athens, Greece. To find more information about the mission, works and activities of the Society and/or to place an order, please visit our website:
www.megas-seirios.gr

or contact us at:
9, Sarantaporou Street, Athens, Greece, P.O.: 111 44
e-mail: info@megas-seirios.gr
Tel.: +30 210 20 15 194
Tel./Fax: +30 210 22 30 864

Translation from Greek: Maria Kourneta

Cover and book design: Marianna Smyrniotou

To Humanity,
who has been struggling
throughout centuries
to express its magnificent nature.

ଔ

CONTENTS

PREFACE

The whole of life is a myth, a bewildering, but also nightmarish dream. A myth with incredible expressions, weaving the course of life, making all of its living beings interact with each other.

Mindless beings or beings with mind, living in ignorance or in knowledge, small and enormous ones, living for a shorter or a longer time. Some with wild instincts and passions, others with high ideals and goals. And the human being, the hero of life's dream, is guided by it towards the course he or she should follow.

A course sometimes pleasing and at other times bringing pain; a course which might be understood or, on the contrary, it might seem incomprehensible and hard to real-ize it in deed.

Life gives to a person the potential to realize one's in-dividuality; it bewilders one with its existence and makes him or her develop an attachment to oneself. And one is vibrated and pulsated by what he experiences through his ego, but when he is overly attached to it – running the risk of giving it some monstrous dimensions – life asks him to renounce it and sacrifice it for others. Then, the person begins to seek the pulse of existence in a certain "we", in some group, and afterwards he spreads his mind even further, thinking of the others' good. He deals with everybody for some time, he is interested in him or her; but soon, he gets tired of the big crowd with its countless forms and their numerous needs. For once more, he iso-lates himself from the world, he loses touch with it, being defensively shut up inside himself to find protection from any real or imaginary perils he thinks he is in. Neverthe-less, this deliberate isolation does not satisfy him for long either, and he again begins to seek contact with the other, with the others, with the whole of humanity.

What life profoundly asks from a person is not to lose one's ego, but to broaden it by including all others in it. And while one wants to respond to its request he or she cannot achieve this because one insists on sustaining his separate existence, the one he was raised and learned to live with. His desires are confused, causing him agitation, insecurities and conflicting desires. He wonders what he is. Is he one person? Is he two? Is he many? His ignorance torments him, he reacts to what he experiences, he resists and, in the end, he gets angry with life itself, with its conflicting demands. He is opposed to the myth that teaches him to be something special and then asks from him to abandon separateness and become one with the whole.

Individual and group. Human and humanity. One and everyone. The confinement to the individual is nightmarish and enchanting at the same time. It is nightmarish because it leads to solitude and enchanting, because it feeds the need to maintain personal ego. The union with others is frightening, since it demands sacrifice, but it is also a release, because it brings fulfillment and gives the sense of safety and security shared by the people who belong to a group.

Is there any golden mean then? Is there any middle way that establishes the existence of both the individual and the group? Can a person be both himself or herself and the others at the same time? Would it suffice to communicate with others, but always make sure one maintains his or her ego? Or does communication inevitably lead to the ego's loss? And what does such a loss mean, what does it benefit and why should it occur? Or perhaps it doesn't exist, but is another one of the strange episodes in the myth of life?

Countless questions emerge from the mind. New ideas are constantly generated, sometimes encouraging and at other times discouraging one in seeking the truth. Moments come when a person completely forgets oneself and studies the problems the others have, society's events, the expressions of the whole of life. His difficulty to understand the deep causes and the meaning of the occurrences disappoints him. He sees the merciless needs he and the others have, their will to function towards their personal gain; he also sees humanity's sole need to function as a harmonized totality. He observes people's opposite wills, their desire to become couples and form families, but also their need to stay alone, both creating enormous difficulties in their substantial union. And all these intensify one's own difficulties to understand and reach union.

The thinking person observes everything that is happening inside and around him. He observes, he communes with himself and reaches some conclusions leading him to respective decisions, each time influenced by the knowledge and the experiences he has. And then he begins to carry out the decisions he has reached. He isolates, he interacts, he participates, he unites, he opposes and experiences his actions' positive and negative effects. And the myth of life keeps on until the hero learns to play his composite role in every level of his existence. Being himself, but also being the others as well. Being the individual, but also being the group. Everyone and the one in absolute harmony. The person who reaches this realization passes to another dimension of consciousness. For him the myth of life ceases, the enchanting and nightmarish dreams end and their position is taken only by the truth. What remains is the substance of life, its simplicity in the phenomenal complexity of its multiple aspects.

In this dimension of consciousness there is neither individual nor group, there is only life itself that is everything. There is only the entity that is everyone and one; it is every individual and group-ego forming the one Ego, the one reality. It is the chosen ones that pass to this dimension, those who chose the whole and are chosen by it, when they prove in deed the firmness of their choice. A choice that the entity itself has infused as a potential within all of us and it just waits for us to seek it, so that it may reveal itself. It waits, but it also trains us to find it, giving us all the stimuli we need to wake up from the dream of "I", from the dream of "we" and from the dream of the group and completely unite with it, become one with it. It is an utmost goal, a supreme one, attained only by constant passages of consciousness from the small ego to the greater one, to the utmost, to the supreme. And when the final passage occurs, the redeemed person, the Saint, the adept, the wise person exclaims the truth with his whole being and his exclamation convulses the universes:

"What individual? What group? What humanity? God is the only one that exists!"

"One is everything and nothing at the same time."

Plotinus

HUMANS AND THE SELF

Man explores "Man". He has done so for centuries... He explores his nature, his origin, his form and its qualities. He uses science in the service of his exploration and defines it as anthropology, biology, medicine, psychology. One plays with all forms of art so as to express and depict human body, one's feelings and thoughts. He uses all historical knowledge, every philosophical theory and every religion to find the responses to his questions. He comes to certain conclusions, rejects certain views, cross-checks some others and, dauntlessly, he continues his research. Essentially, it is one's self one wishes to know through all these preoccupations; it is his or her self that one seeks everywhere; in one's ancestors, in contemporaries, even in one's descendants. The human end is a sacred one, the search for one's identity; because only when a person knows who he is will he be able to let his entity emerge.

What is a human being? Is there an answer to this question which can satisfy everybody? Certainly not, since one person thinks of a human as an impermanent and mortal being, another believes that he is an immortal one, while a third believes in the existence of successive embodiments. Some consider that the human being is the evolutionary descendant of the ape and others say that the human comes from extraterrestrial beings that once inhabited our planet; there are people who recognize that a person is good by one's nature, whereas others see in him or her nothing but weaknesses and maliciousness. How is it, then, possible to have an answer that covers such opposing views, without it being considered as erroneous, limited or dogmatic? Opposing views often encumber and inhibit the efforts to seek truth instead of aiding and encouraging them.

Nevertheless, the inquiring human nature and its great need for knowledge still exist and will always exist, until the day the question "what is a human being" is answered along with many other questions. Providing an answer is not enough however; it must be also heard and, most importantly, it must be confirmed by human

consciousness as being the right one. In the past, replies have been provided by evolved beings that had this
knowledge. Their words, though, have been ignored, misinterpreted, forgotten or accepted only by few, since all
the rest had not been ready to listen, or they did not
want to. The knowledge of the wise has not been assimilated and, for this reason, most people today lead their
life without yet knowing their own self. They keep searching for it in various ways, searching for the truth. Where
must they turn in order to find it and how is its validity
to be affirmed within them?

It is within the self that the answer about the self lies,
it is the self that provides us with all affirmations. The
knowledge about the person and one's true nature exists
in the person itself. Of course, it exists in various other
things as well, like science, philosophy and in the studies of the origin and the evolution of the human race.
Yet, these are individual elements, interpretations of the
essence and not the essence itself. The essence lies only
in the depths of the self and it is there each one should
be immersed in order to know it. Studying emotions or
thoughts, or observing the body is not enough in order
to claim that one knows who he or she is, since these are
minimal fields of consciousness of the whole. They are
generated by the self's essence, they are formed by it, but
they are not its pure being.

May we claim that the human being is only one thing and not many? Could we say a person is immortal even though the body dies? Could we say one is mortal, although there are so many proofs of his or her immortal hypostasis? Isn't it natural to accept that one is immortal on one level and mortal on another one? Can we believe that one only has what we call kindness even though he or she expresses so many of the so called forms of "meanness", or, on the contrary, that a person is only mean, when at times one expresses an unbelievable magnificence of soul? Why not accept the coexistence of all of one's aspects and manifestations? But if we accept that a human being is all these oppositions like littleness and greatness, mortality and immortality, as well as many others, we are automatically led to the next question: "Where do the opposites derive from and why do they exist?"

At this point, searching does not lead to tangible and specific conclusions able to be interpreted by logic. The search is an inner one; it is a personal experience and only the one having it may also understand it. The reason for which opposites exist lies beyond mental interpretations and analyses; it lies in the formless field of the mind. It is the unexplored field of research that no one can search; one may only pass to it and unite with it. Not to be identified with the notions of good and evil, not to be influenced by death and immortality, but to become the essence that generates everything: aspects, powers, ideas and every form. To realize and experience essence everywhere, not only in its formless field, but in its countless opposite expressions as well.

The essence of things is like the taste of foods. Anyone wishing to experience it has to taste it, first letting it overwhelm him or her and then assimilating it with one's whole being. No description is able to transmit the experiencing of essence to the person who deeply refuses to accept it, just like it happens with everything one chooses to know only superficially, denying or overlooking their more profound meaning. One says that a food is salty and another one that it is sweet and is limited to the impression one has of these, paying little or no attention at all to the fact that they both perform the same work: they stimulate taste. He, also, says that something is pleasant and something else is unpleasant, overlooking the fact that both are stimuli given to one's physical, emotional or mental field. He does the same for everything, limiting them to the impression they give him, to certain positive or negative reactions they cause him and, thus, loses the profound consciousness they lead to.

A person wants something or does not want it, is afraid of the difficulties of life or dares to confront them; is happy or sad about what is happening and at this point one usually stops the contact with his or her self. He ceases it in the ascertaining of one's manifestations and does not seek the deeper nature from which all oppositions derive. One turns to it only when some life experiences overwhelm him or her so much, that one needs an interpretation about the necessity of their existence. And it is then, and only then, that truth begins to be revealed, to realize that all share the same purpose, that the only reason for which they exist is to wake us up out of ignorance and lead us to knowledge.

What knowledge does a person acquire from illness, failure, unhappiness, fear but also from health, success, happiness and fearlessness? The knowledge of the self and only this. The knowledge about one's nature constantly transmitted to the person by its own being creates successive stimuli to the unconscious. The knowledge that the human entity is an unbreakable aggregate of countless aspects; the fact that it also is the deep consciousness of these aspects, their essence and hypostasis. In order to know this hypostasis it is necessary to accept all aspects, to experience the positive or negative stimuli they cause to a person, to accept the ones he or she likes and those one does not like alike. Until a person passes to absolute acceptance of all, ceasing to pursue what is pleasant and repulsing the unpleasant, he or she does not unite with one's aspects, being thus unable to know them. Consequently, one remains in a state of ignorance about one's nature as well, the nature of the self, of one's entity.

There are people who realize that they have got a body, a soul and a spirit; others see their needs, their emotions and their thoughts. How many realize, though, that they must embrace all these so that they themselves may become the parts of their self? To become the complete monad, to become what they really are even if they do not realize this? A person is a monad, a composite one, consisting of countless other monads, which compose certain groups that in their turn compose some larger ones. Groups of cells or organs, groups of emotions and thoughts, groups of energies and powers. How can we reach the realization that a monad is formed by totals and subtotals, by groups and lesser monads? How can we see that it is also something beyond all these, the power existing in everything? This power is not revealed to the person who rejects some parts of oneself and desires some others depending on the "coloring" one gives them. It is revealed only to the one who recognizes that every thing is a lesser power, a limited expression of the one infinite power that generates everything. Thoughts, emotions and body are all small powers but they are also full of the same, one and only power field that is diffused everywhere, within everything.

The passage of consciousness from the part to the whole is difficult and we keep on dividing our nature or limiting it only to some of its aspects. And as long as we function this way our self is lost in self-confinement, imprisoned by ourselves due to ignorance. The self is lost; it constantly suffers, receiving stimuli from the aspects it has not yet accepted, asking to be assimilated by its being, to return to the power of the initial source from which they have been generated in the existent world. This is a process leading to redemption even though it passes through resistances and pain. A process ending in the essence, liberating and emerging the true self.

A person is a monad but he or she is also a group at the same time. His or her nature is one within its multiple faces. When one realizes the truth about the self then one will adore all of the aspects, the lesser powers of one's uniqueness. He will not be reversing them out of ignorance, turning them into meanness, pain, passions, insecurities and unhappiness but will see them as parts of the self. And these will not attract anymore, neither will they repulse as one will be united with them. All these will be simply expressions of the person's own power, and they will be directed, they will act and exist following his or her will for existence. A will absolutely united with the entity's will that is one's true nature. Then, the human being, in both essence and form, will consciously be one; one will be the monad, the person will be himself or herself respectively.

THE COUPLE

All other people are every person's mirror. From the moment he is born, a person seems to be in a magic place with a lot of mirrors around him, showing himself from every side. Opposite him, next to him, behind him, at short or further distances, acting like mirrors, clear or dim ones, all people reflect a beautiful or an ugly aspect he has.

There are even times when one of these aspects seems distorted to him, as he would be reflected in a convex or concave mirror that convulses his image. And then he reacts, he becomes ironic towards what he sees, or he is scared and takes flight.

A person does not easily recognize himself in others; he rarely accepts what they show him as attributes of his own, and even more rarely does he accept them, on occasions when what he sees gives him the impression of something unpleasant, unnatural or confusing. One usually claims that he has nothing to do with any paradox or negative behaviors the others express. In case the opposite occurs and the aspects he sees in others appear to be better and nicer than his own, then, his reactions change and vary. Sometimes, he wants to imitate them, at other times he doubts that he may resemble them some day, or he gets attached to them in order to draw out their beauty, their power and their kindness, thus remaining in a position of enfeeblement and lack of will.

Among the crowd existing around any person there is a person who becomes his magnifying mirror. This person is his or her partner with whom one shares a special relationship, something more particular and more different from what one shares with other people. So close a relationship that every part of him in all of its manifestations becomes more and more obvious, more and more clear. Physical features, emotional fluctuations and mental functions constantly appear during the daily contact between the two partners and, therefore, all these are often magnified and seem huge. Thus, an unimportant flaw may become a serious barrier in their relationship or, on the contrary; a virtue may be overestimated due to its frequent exposure.

Man and woman act as a magnifying mirror for each other, not because of their close relationship, or the fact that this may last for a number of years, but because of its multifold nature. Their contact is multiple, being physical, emotional, and mental and being a contact between souls as well. It is not only the result of common needs and common aims, but also the result of common responsibilities. And this spherical nature of their contact displays and magnifies all of their aspects, thus magnifying both the problems that some of these cause and the interdependence to which certain others lead them.

To whom else does one show so many parts of himself as he does to his partner? To whom else does one bare his soul even when he does not consciously do so? It is to one's partner that a person reveals his or her body, expresses his erotic passion, but also one's frigidity or incapacity. It is against him or her that one leans with all his weaknesses or him that he supports with his power. It is with him (or with her) that one gets into ecstasy, becomes bewildered or disappointed, living all the ups and downs of life.

It is the endless friction, the many-sided contact that necessarily leads to the revelation of the couple's aspects. In the other person one sees human characteristics that one has not seen even in oneself. He sees them because they are every day in front of him, they are his partner's countless details, the ways one behaves, one's reactions, needs, desires and abilities. He often considers them to be different from those he expresses himself, than those he thinks himself to be. He does not comprehend that all these are elements of human nature and are, therefore, his own attributes as well, even though they remain unexpressed inside him. The time also comes, though, when he realizes the similarities he shares with his partner as he clearly sees his own actions and functions in those of his partner. Sometimes this realization pleases him, while, at other times, it bothers him. His pleasure or his discontent is not only due to the positive or negative effects of these actions on him, but it is also affected by whether the personal attributes revealed to him are positive or negative.

One's partner is not only the magnifying, multifold mirror where he sees only his present. We would say it becomes a "diachronic" mirror, reflecting him as he used to be in the past or as he may become in the future. If there is an age difference between one and one's partner one sees accordingly the youth one has lost or the age that approaches. The same occurs with health issues as an illness or any weakness the other person has may remind him of something he himself has gone through or something he is in danger of. Apart from what relates to physical states, a person often discerns some of his partner's habits or attributes that he or she also used to have, but they no longer characterize him. One also discerns, though, some other attributes, negative or positive, that he may acquire in the future. If he has overcome some weaknesses that the other person continues to express, then it is possible that he shows understanding for their existence; nevertheless, one might also feel impatience and anger that one's partner is in an earlier evolutionary stage. In case the latter has made certain important passages, then he himself obtains a motive to follow him or, in the contrary, he gets disappointed and jealous because one has not been able to reach this level so far. Antagonism plays its part here as well and its results might be the improvement or the exacerbation of the couple's relationship, or of the individual's course, depending on the way it is utilized.

Criticism, comparison, approval and disapproval are all characteristics of every couple's relationship. Many aspects, differences, similarities, small or great contrasts cause to attract or repel each other. The main pole of attraction is the instincts, the desires and the emotional needs; it is the pole of both attraction and repulsion simultaneously, though, when the expected satisfaction is only partly or not at all acquired. A person pursues satisfaction during his whole life and this becomes even more intense in the couple's relationship since one invests in the other much of one's hopes and expectations of feeling complete. This process is normal, it is necessary for human nature and very helpful, but it does not bring resolution.

Completeness, deep satisfaction cannot be offered to someone else, if that person does not work in order to reach it; if he does not make his own amplifications of conscience and if he does not express the will to be liberated from the aspects that torment him and to find redemption. And these are not only the other person's aspects, as he often imagines or wishes to believe; they are his own as well, they are aspects of all the people. In fact, in approving or disapproving one's partner it is himself or herself that one criticizes. It is himself that he accepts or rejects, and it is from him that he utterly asks to receive what he asks from his partner, even unconsciously. And as long as he does not find completeness inside himself, it is natural not to be able to find it elsewhere, but also, not to be able to transmit it to somebody else.

We are speaking of interaction, pairing, living together and marriage. But who gets married to whom, and where does their marriage lead to? Is the holy marriage performed, does the absolute union between all the couple's expressions and the essence take place, or is its union limited to certain fields or sub-fields of the true nature? Holy marriage, supreme; it is the union with everything, with every aspect of our personal self and with every aspect of our partner. The holy marriage is the soul's embracing for each other, until the two become completely one. It is the entity's recognition in all their differences alike, just like in all their similarities as well. It is, finally, the assimilation of their aspects within the depths of the self.

How can somebody reach the holy marriage to his partner if he has not understood and lived its importance, when he has not embraced his own self through his own being, his soul and his spirit? The marriage reaches a certain level of completeness, corresponding to the degree of evolution one has reached in one's conscience as a person. During this evolutionary course, though, marriage plays an essential part; the person is substantially helped to advance to completeness, as he is being trained in the union with his partner, with all his expressions and his particularities.

Until the human race reaches completeness, man pairs with woman and limits their union at the level he is each time aware of. If one pays special attention to the body, then physical satisfaction becomes the main aim of their interaction; if one is characterized by the expression of intense emotions, it is these he or she seeks to express and cover. But, since neither his physical body or his emotions and his thoughts constitute his whole self, the union he performs through these leaves him in a great degree uncovered. Then, what follows are the inevitable disagreements, the distance, the conflicts, and the interest to find another partner, or the complete rejection of every relationship. One chooses solitude to avoid everything that bothers him about the other person, since he does not see that these are within him, deriving from his own being. And for as long as he does not see or does not want to see the truth, the other person remains for him "the other" without becoming his complement, his continuation, his broader self.

The marriage of the formless internal self to all aspects is the holy couple. It is the union that consciously exists in superior ontological fields and which a person is being trained to reach, along with the whole of humanity. It is the coexistence of the opposites that eternally interact, unite, counteract and, in the end, are assimilated by the essence. When assimilation is completed, then the opposites are regenerated by their essential nature so as to play again the game of life, the game of the countless couples with the many aspects.

This is what every human couple is; the formless and every form, but it is not aware of this truth. Until this realization comes, one thinks he or she gets simply married to another person and due to one's ignorance one limits him or her to what one knows about the other, to what one desires to give or to receive from him or her. One does not see the divine nature in the other person, since he does not see it in himself; or, he sees it only as he imagines it to be and not as it is: absolute, complete, and autonomous. One does not see the Entity in everything and, thus, he confines himself only to certain aspects and to certain aspects of his or her partner as well, both to the ones one likes and to the ones that displease him.

And the mirroring of each other continues along with each other's approval and criticizing, until knowledge is born. A knowledge generated by experience, friction and resistances, by the countless interactions between the aspects. When knowledge comes, the person, as the complete being finally, will not see someone he or she desires or someone he depends on in one's partner. He will see in him the entity as well, which is one within everybody and everything. Then his marriage will be complete, holy, it will be what it substantially is, two completely united in the one. And this one will now consciously give eternal rebirth to itself, bringing out its infinite minor expressions, playing with them like parents do with their children. It will play and train them to become themselves, to become their entity as well. To become the person monad-group, the couple monad-group, but also the broader totality, the humanity monad-group.

THE FAMILY

Man and woman unite, multiply and become three, four, five. Great is the desire of both to see the offspring of their love, the realization of their union. A desire innate in all people throughout the centuries. Everyone wants to see offspring, to take care of him or her, love and give their child everything they have with the hope and the belief that he or she will become better than them. They want their labours to be justified, not only for the good of their child, but also for the good of all humankind, as something in the depths of themselves speaks to them of the importance of evolution, of the necessity for each generation to be better than the previous one. Something in the depths of themselves, also, tells them that, while helping their child to become good and strong, then, many of their imperfections and the errors they have made out of weakness or ignorance will cease tormenting them. Their conscience will find peace and fulfilment, because they will have made a creative work, they will have the proof of their power and love standing alive in front of them.

The upbringing of the child begins with determination and optimism, but also with anxiety and inhibitions. Parents wonder: will they achieve their goal or not? Will the child respond to what they offer to him or her? And is the way they raise it the right one or are they repeating mistakes they have made both towards themselves and towards each other?

Ignorance causes stress, and this complicates the way parents act; their doubt inhibits the expression of love and the first negative effects of their fears begin to be reflected on the child. Then, guilt appears threatening, anxiety grows and the vision for a better offspring seems to collapse, before even being realised. The parents' efforts in such moments would be wasted, if the power of love left them without any aid. Love, however, intervenes constantly, filling their hearts and giving them the will and power to continue their work, to accept even failure; to work with faith to overcome it, transmuting it into success.

The small group called a family has for centuries made efforts to become the solid structure on which wider social groups and the entire human race will find support. The force contributing to its establishment, but, also, the weakness which leads it to its destruction have not yet become sufficiently conscious for the human being. Usually these are sought in the environment, in heredity, in relatives, or even in the partner; little does one wonder whether they exist within one and what one's share of responsibility for building a family or taking it apart might be. Besides, this is very natural, since one is only aware of a small part of his or her power, and as one has seen and accepted very few of his or her weaknesses.

Life educates a person on the knowledge of his nature in every way; in this very same knowledge one is also educated by his active participation in the family circle. As one becomes a father or a mother and is confronted with the physical weakness of children, one is forced to express greater power and will to cover them. This expression of his proves that there are many hidden powers, simply awaiting one's will to be externalised. A person also learns – through his descendants' weaknesses and needs – to be more tolerant when dealing with the weaknesses of others, as well as those of his partner and himself. Gradually, one's viewpoint towards the concepts of "power" and "weakness", "perfection" and "imperfection" begins to change, and through this change the person's consciousness of the complex human nature also widens. Are, however, our education and our evolution the only reasons family exists for? And if this is the case, how different is the education we receive from our family from the one we receive from other groups?

If we would like to listen to various views posing the question: "Why is the institution of family created and maintained?" we would definitely get many different answers. These would be influenced by each person's personal experiences, one's knowledge of human nature and one's general education as well as by one's religious beliefs. Someone would say that family is necessary, because only in its context may one develop true interest and love; someone else would attribute its existence solely to the instinct of reproduction, a third one would see it as a necessity for raising children and someone else would consider it as a failed institution, advocating that it has to be disbanded. The replies to our questions could have been many more and, most likely, all would contain some truth. None, however, would reflect the whole truth, if it was to cover only one or more of the human being's levels.

Human consciousness is multi-layered and so is the purpose of the family, where all the consciousness fields of its members meet and coexist. While that same interaction also occurs in other groups, it is especially evident within the family due to the special relationships of its members, often manifesting itself in a very visible form. There is heredity and the bonds of relation that unite people with each other. There are their common needs, a common place of residence, their common interests, even their common habits. All these contribute to the family members' coming in close contact, in multiple areas of their existence. They are physically present in the same house for many hours or even constantly. Their emotional responses influence one another incessantly. Their thoughts are transmitted through words and actions, or even intuitively from one to another. Parents, children, siblings but also other family members form a set of very strong bonds. Bonds naturally giving everyone a sense of unity and security, unless they lead to oppression and coercion.

Based on the above, it is obvious that the family undertakes a great work aimed at developing group consciousness among its members, constantly offering them the opportunity to express it. However, the interaction of all those mentioned so far is not enough for forming a group consciousness, since these are nothing but parts of human nature; nor is it sufficient to address and resolve the problems that they might create. Only if all fields of consciousness are identified and interact, is the family able to express the real group. This is rarely achieved, or it is accomplished only to some extent and not definitely, since many parts of the human being are most of the time ignored or overlooked. People's spiritual nature is ignored, the reference to their deeper self, their ontological existence. Hence difficulties in families are only temporarily resolved; they often reappear in the same or in a different form and, thus, the collective consciousness's development is not completed.

The lack of reference to the ontological nature causes many problems, because it confines the family members to the consciousness levels they are already aware of. And these are for everybody – with the exception of very spiritually advanced persons – the body, the emotions and the mind, which one seeks to satisfy and develop further. Although such care is necessary, it is not sufficient as it is evident by the results existing so far in the progress of the family; a progress that educates people on broadening their consciousness, truly uniting with each other and becoming an inseparable group.

The contribution of the family institution to the development of group orientation is particularly important, because family is not only what it seems to be, it is not merely some individuals of both sexes at different ages sharing family bonds. It's also a totality of fields of consciousness, which all together form the one collective consciousness, lying within all of its fields and subfields and including them in its own range as well. If we were to parallel the consciousness' fields with the persons' biological ages we would see that they accurately reflect them, although the people themselves may not consciously express them. Briefly, we would say that a nursling symbolizes the awakening of consciousness out of ignorance, an infant reflects the development of an initial physical consciousness, whereas a child symbolizes the need for knowledge accumulation; a teenager is a symbol for the desire to exchange and augment what has been already conquered and an adult personifies the maturity transferred to more immature fields. There is, also, the embryo, namely the absolute ignorance, the "sleep" of the unconscious and, finally, the old man, symbol of wisdom, fulfilment and synthesis of all previous fields of consciousness.

There are periods of time in a family during which individuals of all biological ages, from a fetus to an old man, are included in it; this is the natural expression of the symbols corresponding to all fields of consciousness. But, even if this never occurs and a family consists of people of one or two ages, the fields of consciousness are all included within the persons, although they might not be aware of this fact. Within each member there are simultaneously the unconscious and the wisdom just like there is every infant, teenage and adult aspect. It is not easy to realize the aspects' coexistence, since we have not yet attained wisdom, that is, we have not become "elders" yet, with the profound significance of the concept. For this reason, the family institution comes to bring out all levels of our nature that we can not see otherwise. The infant's ignorance, the child's stubbornness, the adolescent's drive are easy to understand when observed in our children; then we may learn to see them within us as well. To the extent possible, our perception of the concept of the family begins to differentiate. We gradually realize that we can not restrict it to a group of relatives, to a group of interdependent people sharing certain needs, emotions and thoughts, as a family it is in fact something beyond all this; it is an aggregate of fields of consciousness.

We speak of affinity, looking for it in bonds of blood, because we cannot or we do not want to acknowledge it in our affinity with the soul of the world. We rely on our relationship with our relatives, because we have not learned to rely on the union with every person's profound self. We refer to our natural families alone, because we are not aware of our spiritual connection with them. All these exist; ties of blood, relatives and families, but they are not themselves consciously the essence; they are only its expression. They have not become profoundly conscious of things and of themselves; they are simply aspects. As long as we function in this way, confined to aspects, manifestations and personalities, without discerning the essence within them, family problems will continue and will be transferred from one generation to another.

Periods of time come during which the family institution reaches a remarkable level of development. Soon, however, it sways back, being in danger of alienation. It is reconstructed, making new efforts to achieve a more integral form without, though, making a substantial change in its base and, thus, any difficulties encountered lead it to a new crisis. Every crisis is another stimulus, an impetus forcing us to look for the cause of the difficulties elsewhere, so as to be able to overcome them permanently and completely. And the reason lies in our ignorance of what family really is, of what it personifies, embodies and represents. This is no other but the divine field within us, within our family members and within all the families of the world.

In the highest divine level family is the absolute; it is the one field of consciousness with all its fields and subfields. What is asked from us is not to reach the absolute instantly in order to be able to experience the divine part of our family as people, but to simply acknowledge the existence of the absolute in every person of our family circle. To acknowledge it in infants, in the elderly and in ourselves without being affected by their weak and negative expressions. This acknowledgement, beginning as a simple consideration, is the first big step towards the change of the family institution's base. A change made through differentiation of attitude towards everybody, accepting the field of consciousness each one expresses, having faith in the fact that everybody moves forward to reach union with the divine that never ceases to lead their course, since it exists within them, being their very own self.

This is the step that must now be taken by the group-family. It must broaden its mind and its heart, always referring to its inner nature, so that it may one day become what it really is; to become the essence and the depiction of the divine family. Repeating circles already made; rotating on the same limited unstable base, continually swayed by people's emotions and needs, all these serve no purpose. Good is the only base of every family and society, embracing all fields and subfields of needs, while firmly remaining in the position of love and offering. When this becomes understood, the family's course will change and family members will be steadily directed towards the emergence of the good that is the true nature of all beings.

THE WILL
TO FORM GROUPS

There are two wills guiding a person during his life, directing him in every step he takes as an individual and integrating him in certain groups. The person is not aware of one of these wills, he does not know it exists; he just follows its directions fully or partly and some-times with a significant reaction. This will is the will of the ontological self, the will of the entity which is diffused everywhere and within him as well. It is this that defines his family, his country of origin and his race. The human being – not being consciously united with his ontologi-cal nature – cannot understand the reason for being a member of a particular family, country or race. He takes them for granted, whether he likes them or not and, usually, he is little or not at all concerned with the deeper causes of their existence. He is raised in the groups he was born in, and only if they exercise great pressure on him, will he become rebellious and distance himself from their influence.

The second will, leading a person to become a member of a group, is also realized by him at some level. It is his personal ego's will, which he knows quite well and therefore he is aware of its will. Even when he does not understand the real motives of his desires, he knows with whom he wants to come in contact, and whom he wishes to avoid; to which group one wishes to belong and which one displeases him. Even though the will of personal ego performs significant work, it is much more limited than the ontological ego's will. The individual's satisfaction, his own personal development and the covering of his own needs are its primary purposes. On the contrary, the ontological will is infinite, including every personal will and aiming at the harmonious coexistence and spiritual evolution of all people.

The two wills do not often coincide. The personality's will is often carried away by its egocentric aim; it gets overly inflated, crosses its natural limits, thus coming into conflict with the will of the Entity. Only when its aim becomes a broader one – if a person's consciousness has come to a respective expansion – does its will begin to harmonize with the Entity's will and aim at the collective good. And this does not always occur consciously; one does necessarily realize that his interest in other people expresses a broader ontological field. Even so, his actions prove that there has been a change within him. This change may bring the next stage of consciousness, if it remains stable, and let the knowledge of the ontological self develop. When this happens one begins to consciously work for the harmonization of his or her individual will with the ontological will aiming at one's personality's integration in the work of the whole.

One of the basic problems caused by a person's personality is the difficulties one has in relationships with others, in one's cooperation with them and in the development of the group spirit. Often, in the groups to which one belongs, the personal wills of the members come into conflict with each other, resulting in inhibition of the achievement of the common goal. Nevertheless, one still longs to belong to a group; he or she wants to be social, cooperative and to produce some group work.

If we seek to find where this desire comes from, we will see that its source exists deep within human nature. It is not the will of one person alone, it is not the need of some people, but of the entire humanity; it is a will common to everybody. Its unknown great power guides the human being in every way, to unite with the group and, in order to push him to advance to this union, it brings him into the world small and powerless, dependent on others. The same has always been happening, even when the Earth's population was very small, when the word was still in primitive stages of development, and contact among people was limited to a rudimentary communication among them. The same occurs today, when mental development has advanced, the word has developed, and communication takes place through a number of different means.

All these realizations lead to the conclusion that the will to form groups and function within them lies beyond any human desires; it is an urge given to us in order to be integrated in a group and this urge cannot be avoided. Its power comes to overwhelm the person with vehemence, forcing him to break the barriers of his consciousness and unite with others. This impetus is nothing but the current of Life itself, the current of the soul, the one Soul of the entire humanity, the Soul of the whole universe. It is its very own power that passes through all people, it takes with it all the extra energies of the soul that they insist on keeping inside their own individual out of fear of deprivation, and it spreads them all around to everybody. And then it calls them to acknowledge it everywhere, to see and realize its existence; to realize the one Soul existing within every person, every group, within the whole of humanity.

Soul means love; soul means wisdom. Soul is the energies and the powers overwhelming the universe, giving life to bodies, connecting them with each other and maintaining the balances among them. These are what urge a person to grow up, to expand one's consciousness, to see that he or she is not only one person but many, a group, an aggregate. They urge him to break ego's bonds, unite with his soul's nature, and live the experience of bliss that can be experienced only through diffusion and expansion, only through the expression of love.

A person cannot easily accept the power of the Soul; he cannot directly follow its flow. The seed for group life is deeply rooted within him though, constantly growing and asking to be expressed. Not knowing how to express it through his soul, he expresses it according to his own level, and begins to form social groups within his own, personal boundaries. The groups are turned into organizations, professional unions, political parties and charity institutions, or even groups for excursions, dancing and recreation. Sometimes, he gets so distant from the initial will of the Soul that his groups – instead of giving life and bliss to himself and others – become cores of criminality and destruction. All these functions are fields of the personality as it is not yet united with the power of the Soul. It is a phenomenal group mentality that never leads to the essence of the group; it never brings love and wisdom into light.

The human being's error does not lie in the fact of organizing recreational groups, political parties and different unions. The error lies in the fact that one does all these without Soul, without true love and interest in others. Even when a person believes and claims that he or she wants to aid the society, it is the ego he deeply wishes to satisfy most of the time. He wants to attend a group, to feel he belongs somewhere, to feel useful. He wants to appear good, great, worthy, to be recognized by the others and create a circle of funs around him. It is for this reason that so many group efforts fail, distancing themselves from their initial goal and becoming one more means for a great egocentric function. Rare are the cases when personal needs are left aside, leaving the pure will of the entity in their position; leaving the current of the soul that expands to the work that has to be performed without any obstruction.

The fight between the two wills continues; a fight that always begins from one's limited aspect, from the personality that is still evolving. Because the Entity does not fight against anybody, since it is everything and everybody. This is also the personality, the hidden wisdom, the mirroring of the infinite ontological ego in one single person, but also in an infinite number of persons. Until the "person" understands what his true nature is, the entity teaches him or her the truth in countless ways. It encourages him or her to form groups, even if the groups share egoistical aims, because through these one realizes one's mistakes and eventually asks to be redeemed from their consequences. Then what a person needs is given to him and this is the current of love that had always been offered to him, but he refused to accept it out of fear or ignorance.

This is what the group needs to become a real group: it needs love and interest, it needs the Soul. This is the only thing able to develop the group spirit and let the pure will of the Entity express itself. Everything else, any other effort for forming groups and functioning within them is but a simple pre-stage for the forming of the substantial group. Pre-stages that, if not evolved, might end in the complete reversal of the notion of the "group". They might reinforce the egoistical, egocentric will of personality even more, and not let it express its wisdom, thus intensifying its unconscious or conscious fight with the Entity.

In reality, a group is not formed by personalities as long as the latter remain in the expression of an attitude of separateness and do not pass to the substantial group mentality and function. Only the personalities' assimilation to the group's entity may bring the true group into light. And when the group passes into light – expressed by the eternal flow of the soul's power from one person to another – then it is revealed to it that all people are One. This is the knowledge people seek, the knowledge of the

One, the absolute unity of all. The unity is the one which, by its hidden will, urges them to form groups and participate in them, even while making countless mistakes, until they achieve their final aim, which is to break the barriers of separateness. And when they pass to union they can consciously adopt whatever personality the others need, in order to educate them in the profound sense of the group, in its essence, the nature of the One.

PARTICULARITY AND UNIQUENESS

Nature gives every person a certain particularity, a special attribute that is exclusively his or hers. It is the one different element that does not exist in anybody else, including one's twin brother or sister. It is as if nature aims to point out to a person that among the group one still remains an individual, even if what makes him distinct from the others might be something infinitely small. This attribute might be a difference in height or weight, in the way he moves or expresses oneself or an emotional response.

Countless are the individuals that humanity consists of and each one is unique and unrepeatable. Variety is such that our mind is unable to conceive it, understand it and assimilate it.

Apart from the different attributes, nature gives people many common elements as well that automatically categorize them into certain groups. Big groups or smaller ones, groups in which people remain until the end of their life, and others from which they depart throughout the course of time. The sort of these groups is such that they are not even considered to be groups. The first and greater group is the one defined by sex dividing the earth's population into men and women. The second one is the race to which each person belongs, regardless of one's sex. And the third group is our age to which we belong for a certain time, regardless of our race or our sex. This categorizes us into children, adults and elders.

All these three attributes, sex, race and age, are directly connected to our physical form, to our body, which also has some other elements, though, making us belong to smaller groups. These groups are the beautiful and the ugly, the tall and the short, the fat and the thin, as well as those who have a special talent, certain rare physical abilities, or on the contrary, certain difficulties. The way, in which common human elements are met and combined, forms a person's exclusive attributes, offering him his distinctiveness, that unrepeatable something that makes him or her special. No matter how hard one might search around him he won't find his perfect match, his identical self; he cannot discover in any other person an absolutely faithful depiction of himself.

Each human being is unique, an individual with an exclusiveness, an expression of nature; it seems unrepeatable, as if nature wishes to continually express a new aspect, a new element. The person, as if he realizes the will of the nature that created him, uses the distinctiveness given to him for the maintenance of his individuality. Simultaneously, though, he seeks the similarities he shares with the others both in form and in the attributes of character and personality as well as in all other partial qualities he has. One needs to know that he belongs somewhere, that he is a man or a woman, black or white, a child or an elder. This categorization gives him a new distinctiveness, the one of the group he belongs to. A group ego develops in his consciousness, following a parallel course with the individual ego. The group wants to maintain its separate position within the whole, the position giving it its special attribute. At the same time, though, it wants to expand, to integrate in a greater group and become the group-humanity.

Nature's game seems like a game of segregation and synthesis. It separates and categorizes into kinds, genders, races, but it also makes a synthesis of all these in the one kind, the one race, the human one. A game that complicates a person as it creates in him two different wills; the one making him invest on his particularity and the other making him be disturbed by it. No mater how much one understands that life would be monotonous and, possibly, very difficult, if every person wasn't different from the others, one often realizes that the differences do not offer only a pleasant variety, but that they also cause enormous problems And then one wonders what is the purpose of particularity, what nature seeks to succeed by its diversity, and what this nature is, after all.

All people do not have the same interest in such questions; many people simply surpass them and try to live the best way they can both as individuals and as members of a group. Nevertheless, even the people who deal with these do not always find satisfactory responses, neither do they reach similar conclusions; some people consider the existence of similarities and differences as a coincidence, others attribute it to heredity, whereas there are also some who see it as a combination of matter's molecules. Certain people recognize in them the expression of a will that gave life and shape to the human form, while a percentage of people accept its work without any resistance and some criticize it for the imperfections of its creatures.

Nature remains uninfluenced by the positive or negative reactions of people. It continues the work of its creation and it shapes them, as it shapes all beings, giving them distinctive characteristics, but also a number of common elements as well. All these are nothing but the externalization of its own will, the natural manifestation of its infinite power. Because nature is not anything different than the power of life, as creation is not disconnected from the creative principle that shapes it. It is this creation that is projected to its infinite faces; it is this that generates all forms, the multiplicity of the aspects, their antitheses and their similarities. Its breath exists within everything; it is formed and depicted in their bodies, giving them life.

Each person's particularity is a depiction of the Being's uniqueness. The similarities among human forms are a depiction of the one essence, and each small human ego is a depiction of the one Ego. As we are not able to directly realize the uniqueness of the supreme self, of which we are all disciples, our discipleship is made through our distinctive form. This is what gives first the sense of our existence, the sense of the individual, of the particular field we are able to know and realize in our consciousness. In parallel we are disciples of our consubstantial nature, and in order to unite with it eventually, this nature educates us by giving us common attributes and similar characteristics.

We pass from stages of identification with our personal ego and then with a group's ego to gradually pass to the one ontological Ego. Unifying in our conscience the notions of particularity and similarity is a presupposition for this passage. To achieve this, though, it is necessary to give them another breadth, to see them through another dimension. To refer the particularity of the individual to the Being's uniqueness and its similarities with other individuals to the consubstantial nature of all things.

The one Self is unique and unrepeatable within the whole world in every point of the infinite universe. Its nature is one no matter how it is manifested, or how much it is misinterpreted and divided by our limited conscience. Every human being is unique as well, since its essence and its form is the essence and the form of the Being. The existing differences and similarities are not accidental; they are not just consequences of heredity or a synthesis of particles of matter. Heredity, as everything else that intervenes in the shaping of the form and in the characteristics of a human being, is itself a means used by nature to maintain the similarities and to create particularities. This is the way nature educates us for as long as our consciousness is identified with our form. It dissolves identification giving countless stimuli, opposite to each other, all having as their aim to lead us to union with its essence and its uniqueness.

A small ego and an infinite ego is what every person is. One is special, but also unique; alike and consubstantial simultaneously. The limited field of consciousness one has reached keeps him captive of particularities and similarities. The great field of consciousness one potentially is, however, educates him through his bonds to grow up, expand and become more familiar with it. Similarities along with existent diversity are all the indescribable wisdom, the infinite love. The One's Love for everything and everybody that is the monadic Self.

THE HUMAN RACE

The human race surrounds the entire planet like a great power. A power formed by lesser powers, constantly interacting with each other, building a plexus around the earth. This plexus is not made of bodies, but it is fed by the presence of the bodies from which all energies and powers that it consists of emanate from. The main levels of this energy plexus are three: the first one is the sensual and instinctive, the second one is the emotional and the third one is the mental. These dominate human function as their energies recycle and influence each other without any interruption. Instincts, emotions and thoughts are transferred from one person to another, they spread, and they interact, they are multiplied and absorbed by everybody to be again diffused around them even more powerfully than before.

Directly influenced by the sensational part of themselves, people initially separate themselves into the categories they realize through their senses and into which nature itself has classified them. They are not confined, though, in this classification, they do not separate the races and the genders, or just the children from the elder and the beautiful from the ugly. They extend to other separations, influenced by their emotional and mental level. Preferences, repulsions, appreciation and rejections incite and strengthen each one's innate need to be something special, but also to be part of a group.

Society with its classes and its different groups reflects in some way the physical forms of people, their distinctive features and their similarities. Its reflection, though, rarely depicts nature's wisdom; it usually reverses it, turning it into ignorance, folly or even paranoia. Social groups, if not motivated by true interest for the aggregate of people, and if they do not function through reference to an ontological field, are motivated by egoism, dispute and uncontrollable desires. Thus, their function is worlds apart from the love nature expresses, through the different, but also through the common attributes it gives to people.

Racism, initially starting from race differences, has left the borders defined by form and has created other borders, social ones. Social racism, though, is not confined to people's classification into two or three categories alone. It does not divide them into groups based only on their citizenship or depending on their political views; the formation of groups extends to every level of their existence. Rich and poor, educated and uneducated, clever and silly are all separated from each other at times because they themselves choose this separation and, at other times, because others force them to do so. No matter the efforts made for the existence of an equal attitude towards all people, racism continues to exist, expressed in many ways, further intensifying the already intense problems of the society.

Spiritual people work to convey high ideals and notions; their own messages are also very easily misinterpreted, though, often used in an erroneous way. Thereby we observe the phenomenon of the wrongly self-styled spiritual people who think of themselves as superior, limiting their relationships to those they consider to be like them and avoiding contact with those they consider inferior. The same applies to some artists who often belong to very closed circuits, as they believe themselves to be chosen. Because of this attitude, the group they form loses the true notion of the group, since their goal is, once more, their individual satisfaction. The same thing is pursued by people who are in a position of weakness, like alcoholics, drug addicts or beggars. They, as well, seek to be with those who are like them, because they deeply want to cover an individual need. It is obvious that castes exist everywhere, maybe not consisting of masters and slaves as occurred in the past, but in essence, being equally restrictive since the ones encouraging them or participating in them enslave themselves and others in a limited conception they share of the human being.

Nature reflects the Being's uniqueness in people's distinctive features and Its essence in their similarities. However, it is only the reflection they see that they realize, beginning to imitate and reflect it through their deeds. The natural differences among them, but also their similarities, do not lead them to union; on the contrary, they become the cause for expressing greater separateness and a more egoistical function. It is as if they themselves become the reflection of the truth's reflection, and thereby they become more and more distant from the essence and from their uniqueness. And the problem of separateness grows bigger and bigger as the truth is surrounded by the personalities' needs which, as if they were dense veils of ignorance and fear, hide it deeply in the unconscious without letting it come into light.

The human race struggles within the energy plexus that it builds for itself out of ignorance. It struggles among its desires, its unstable emotions and the countless thoughts that discomfort it. It tries to find peace through them, at times by feeding their needs and at other times by suppressing them. Even so, they do not abate, they never end; on the contrary, they get stronger through constant occupation with them or through denial of their expression. Humanity does not find its true self; it does not become the group it really is, and naturally it does not become the group-monad, the one global, unified field of consciousness.

Efforts are made by a significant number of people to find a definite solution, to get out of the dead-end and live without conflicts and frictions. Valuable works are scheduled, ideas are put into practice and groups are formed to apply them. All these actions are positive and bring certain changes in life. However, rarely are the changes permanent and stable. Soon, new problems appear, being nothing but a new form of the old ones. These always lie in the human function that is limited to the physical, emotional and mental field. An exception to this rule is made by those who leave these levels going over and beyond them; they project a pure will that breaks long established situations, bringing a new breath, a current of power and love.

People are afraid of demise; the demise of the plexus they have been living in for centuries. They are afraid of it because they see it only as a demise and not as broadening and redemption. They remain in a function that could be called horizontal if the energies they transmit one to another in order to recycle with each other were placed on an imaginary level. Often this recycling is limited only to one of these levels, as, at times, it is mostly the body with its sensational needs that vibrates, whereas, at other times, emotions vibrate and, at certain others, mind dominates. But even when these three interact, still, the common level they form is limited, covering only one part of their nature. And this part is the one seeking only impermanent and ephemeral satisfactions, which are soon to be lost as new needs are instantly created. As it always remains voracious and wishes to receive food constantly in order to exist, it cannot substantially help people unite with one another, since it constitutes that part of them that maintains separateness through recycling.

In fact, this function is not a horizontal one. Body, emotions and mind barely let energies diffuse from one person to another, and after doing so they serve again each one's cumulative need for personal satisfaction. Horizontal is only the expression of love that smoothly spreads to everybody, to cover their needs without withholding any of their energies for selfish purposes.

Nature creates human races, genders, the common and the different attributes of people in order to educate us in their unification. And instead of turning them into union, we turn them into hostility, racism, social classes, categories and classifications. We take the lesson through our mistakes until we comprehend the deep meaning of the differences. Until we realize that these exist in order to interact with each other, be lovingly embraced and cease to bother or bewilder us. Until we stop seeking the solution only in some levels of ourselves, which have not brought us the solution until now, and instead go over and beyond these and daringly unite them with the other part of ourselves. To give them the true power of our nature, the power that passes through the whole human race, the vertical power that is grounded within our being and shapes our bodies, its own countless forms. Only if we unite with this power, the plexus of these energies and powers restricting us, previously being a centre of individual needs, will it then differentiate and be transmuted into a radiation of love.

Racial differences, social classes, racism! What might be the role and the power of all these and how can they affect us, when we see the one human race in everything? When in every person we discern Man no matter the form of his body, his wealth, his abilities and his weaknesses. How is it possible to emotionally depend on somebody when we have learnt to truly love him? Why remain in a plexus of uncontrollable energies when we can control them through the pure power nature gives us? It would be unreasonable to maintain such an obsessing and tormenting attitude since truth would have revealed itself to us.

It is for this revelation that each person consciously or unconsciously works. And when this comes his or her mind is illuminated and one experiences truth with his or her whole being. One lives as a person and as a member of a group but is not confined in these as he deeply knows that his self is the whole humanity. He knows that the human race is one, no matter how many forms the people composing it might take; he knows that the human society is one, since its entity is also one. A divine Entity, limitless, united with the entity of the entire universe. It is this that eternally creates all human beings and motivates them to unite with each other, because only such a union will make them unite with it as well. To become the unshakable vertical power that descends to the human race and diffuses its power through it, circling the whole planet with its light.

PEOPLE'S NATURE

Light is the base of the whole life; fiery light, spiritual light. Even when the form of life is just a simple body, an individual, it hides the power of life in its depths. It is the formless power of the spirit existing within all aspects, within every being, big or small, as well as in all of their manifestations. A person's existence is also fiery; it is the finite and the infinite existence, the expanding one, the indivisible.

The light of life descends into darkness, power descends into weakness and knowledge descends into ignorance; they do so to redeem them from their confinement, to make them realize their fiery nature and transmute them into spirit. And a person, being himself the synthesis, the composition of all opposites, uses his or her mind's power and seeks to find the light within the darkness of one's self, within one's form, and discover the fire of the spirit. He acts the same way about everything and everyone as well, because this is the aim of his fiery nature, to lead one to the base of life and make him realize it. A person is not usually aware of his nature's will, nor can he easily discern it, as it is surrounded by countless others wills and desires. But it always exists within him, vibrating him by its fiery power, until his lesser desires settle down, allowing it to be revealed and, finally, unite with it.

All of a person's fields of consciousness are small fires crossed with each other in order to make up his (or her) total spiritual individual. Their interaction though does not easily lead to union, because fires conflict with each other, due to the different roles each one is meant to play. Emotions resist logic, thoughts exercise pressure on desires, and instincts intervene with emotions. Great friction is generated by the constant conflicts, as each level of consciousness, as a small individual being itself, insists on maintaining its individuality and wishes to overwhelm the whole of human consciousness in order to achieve its aim. And a person, not being aware of his pure fiery nature, sometimes charges the fires of the mind and at other times is utterly dominated by the fires of emotions or by the power of his instincts. Then, he himself wonders about his manifestations; he also wonders about who he is and which one of his expressions is his true nature.

It is their true nature that all people seek to find even if they have never wondered about what it is or if they do not even suspect it exists. They cannot avoid such a quest, since they are directed towards it by nature itself, constantly convulsing them by its fire, penetrating every fold of their existence, vibrating them by each lesser fire of its own. And they, – whether they want it or not – respond to its impetus leading them to union with it. The lesser fires' resistances, though, always insisting on overwhelming them, do not let them go deeper in themselves and unite with the one and only fiery nature of their being, of their spirit. As their need for union still exists they turn to other people, trying to interact with them in order to cover their uncovered need. Deep inside, though, they always seek the union with their true nature which they unconsciously hope that the others are aware of, and that they will help them find it.

All of these processes, mostly conducted without any knowledge, may lead a group's members to very intense and often negative expressions. As the fires of the various fields of consciousness of two or more people interact with each other, their power is multiplied. So, as a result of their crossing, instead of bringing the revelation of the one fire, each one of them grows and dominates the individuals even more. Whatever might be manifested by a group is much more exaggerated than what is expressed by a single person. The emotion expressed by a crowd may bring panic or mania; the instinct's passion may lead to orgies. Identification with some ideas may turn them into obsessions, irrational or repressive ones. These fields grow bigger and bigger, as if they wanted to ensure their existence, to defend themselves against the new threat they sense approaching and circling them, in order to dissolve their individuality; against the threat that is no other than the united force of the group, its spiritual field. However, if the group is not yet aware of its fiery nature, it cannot express it, thereby succumbing to its limited fires to which every one of its members separately succumbs as well.

In the individual we see the individual, in the group, we see the group, we discern the respective individual or group manifestations, and, usually it is right there where our ability to discern stops. If we could break the barriers of the form, if we could go beyond the impression we have by both the others' and our own movements, reactions and deeds by using our mind, then a new world would reveal itself to us. We would not be led astray by the small fires, but we would refer everything to the world of the spirit, the world of the fiery nature which is one and consubstantial within everybody and every manifestation.

Fire is every little will we have, every great and lesser need and every desire. Fire that warms us by its presence, waking us from inertia and pushing us to acknowledge the uniqueness of its fiery nature in it as well, in order to relieve it from its separative encasement. All other people's wills are also fire and the same applies for every group's member and for the whole of humanity. We come into conflict with them because we haven't – and neither have they – freed the pure fiery nature hidden in the depths of all our wills. Each one of us has not formed a fiery self, has not become a free spiritual being, the whole of a consciousness of the fields one consists of and, as a result, one cannot let his individual fire be spread to others in order to be substantially united with them.

Discernment is not easy to develop in a person, so that one may penetrate form and see the essence within it. The union with the spiritual hypostasis does not come without struggle and arduous work. It is hard to recognize the depth of things, the depths of people, and the depths of the self. Who could say that he or she acknowledges the current of love in every desire? Who realizes the power that exists in weaknesses? Who daringly penetrates into one's passions, not to be driven away by them but to draw from them the fire that maintains them and return it back to its fiery nature? Finally, who recognizes in everybody their spiritual self, even though they might be in complete ignorance of its existence? And who sees humanity, not only as an aggregate of people, but also as a group of many fires being in an evolutionary process to unite with each other and become the divine fire of the whole wide world?

There is something like a fairy tale saying that each soul leaving this world becomes a star shining on the sky. In fact, the soul always shines, since it is part of the spiritual fire. It also shines when it is inside a human body as long as we are willing to see its light and decide to recognize our spiritual nature in our form and everywhere. We should not expect the physical body's death for the soul's light to be let free, like the fairytale says, but let it shine every moment, penetrating the dense material of the form that hides its blaze behind its needs. Only then will we comprehend that it is the light alone that exists everywhere, the spiritual fire that is the base of life, of every life: individual life, group life, humanity's life but, also, of the life of the universe.

Life would not exist without the divine fire. Without realizing the fact that fire exists, life is not true life, it is just a fantasy, a dream coming for a while and then leaving, lost in the unconscious field of darkness and ignorance. Without the realization that the one fire exists in the body, this is governed by all the other lesser fires it consists of and, thereby, it does not live substantially, it does not exist as a bright spark of its nature. Only complete realization of the spiritual nature within every cell, every organ, in every vibration and in every emotion or thought, is what makes a person a vivid manifestation of the divine fire. It makes him or her a part of its own, a fiery part of the aggregate divine fire.

When a person makes the passage to the deep knowledge of his nature, all people around him become spiritual fires in his consciousness. Only then is he or she able to help them become aware of who they are, to help them unite with each other at a soul level and build the spiritual group, the fiery, spiritual human race. A race whose work is secret as it works to bring the light of the spirit to the whole planet, offering its knowledge and its love to all beings living on it.

HUMANS
AND THE PLANET

Many times a group of people reminds us of the sun with its planets, as one of its members has the position of the centre that diffuses its power to the others who follow him or her coordinated by his directions. This person might be a family's father, an enterprise's manager or a country's governor. It is not accidental that in the past certain kings were called "suns". It was because of the position of power and love that their citizens were asking them to express. The same occurs in our times with the members of a group, as they ask the same thing from the most mature, the most powerful and the most experienced member. If he proves worthy of the position he has, then the group's course is facilitated and its work has many possibilities of positive advance.

Groups are not always formed this way, though. A central person who completely directs others does not exist in every group, or, if somebody arbitrarily takes such a position this is not something permanent and it is not officially recognized by everybody. Most of the times the people included in a group aim at an hierarchical distribution of the obligations and a possibility for everybody to check the others. They all want to participate in the activities aiming at their group's achievement by expressing their opinion and undertaking their share of responsibility towards their common work. In this case there are times that the majority becomes the directive force of the group and times when the group is directed by one or more members, the ones who, for some special reasons, impose their opinion and will.

Apart from these two groups – the one relying mainly on the power of one and the second relying on the interaction of the entire group's powers – there is also a third group-form expressing the absolute reversal of the sun's and his planets' function as its attribute. There is no person having a central position of power spread to the others for the group's benefit. On the contrary, the one holding the position of the centre wants only to absorb power from those being on the circumference, acting like a whirlpool which destroys everything by its whirl. His goal is to constantly feed his ego and enlarge his personality deriving from the members of the group everything they have: their emotions, their ideas and their money. And the members get attached to him, either out of weakness and ignorance or because they do not realize what is happening to them; they do not realize the state of enfeeblement they are in.

Groups in which the central person is egocentric and puts pressure on others are present at every social level. The manifestations of egocentrism are not always obvious or easy to recognize, so that they might be characterized as negative. They are not always as evident as, for instance, in groups of under-aged people who have a drug dealer as their leader, taking advantage of them. Nevertheless, the same function may be expressed everywhere, beginning with a prime minister who sees his ministers only as a means of his own glory, and ending with the member of a family that demands that the others be constantly occupied with him.

This classification of groups into three basic categories also shows the existence of three basic ways in which a person functions. The first one is the diffusion of the soul's energies and powers form one person to others. The second one is the recycling of the energies with them to produce a more integral group work, and the third one is the absorption of the others' power by one, with the only aim to be personally satisfied. These functions depict the three respective fields of consciousness that exist in every person and are part of the total of their consciousness. Their different manifestations are greatly due to the amount of consciousness a person has reached regarding these fields. They are mainly due to the choice one makes regarding the way in which one wants to function, that is, whether he wants to diffuse his powers and recycle them, or to accumulate them within himself.

Being an inhabitant of the planet, a person is naturally influenced by the environment where he or she lives and follows the laws of nature. The planet's dependence on the sun and its rotation around it automatically makes all beings that inhabit it dependent on it; it is from him they constantly receive the needed radiation that is necessary for their life.

The position of the receiver who is not able to survive unless he absorbs energy from somebody or something is not expressed or limited by man to the needs of his physical body. He transfers it from the physical level and he experiences it in every other level of his existence. He wants to be emotionally covered, to acquire knowledge, to be affirmed as a person, to always gain something for himself. In this way he maintains the position of dependence and need for receiving constant feedback from a source of power. This stance though is not only a part of the human field of consciousness; it is always a part of the collective consciousness, since it is the one existing everywhere in the universe and generating all its lesser fields through its countless creatures and, naturally, through human beings as well.

The second level of consciousness, also being part of the collective consciousness, is recycling and the human being is also being trained in it. A person learns from nature itself that he or she must labor, he must offer a part of one's powers, of one's own self in order to enjoy any sort of goods, have food, clothing and residence, but also for having descendants. The recycling one must carry out in the physical field in order to survive teaches a person the respective emotional, mental and soul recycling. In this way one passes to the second level of consciousness of his existence. It is the level of recycling one tries to externalize even when he or she does not realize the effort hiding behind one's actions while one pursues equality to exist among the members of a group, or when one aims at the exchange of their views, the equal distribution of responsibilities, but also everybody's equal rewards from common work.

The deep significance of recycling has not yet been clarified in most people's consciousness and, for this reason, groups find difficulties in realizing it. It is often that one or more of their members function from the previous level, having the need to act always as receivers. The result of this function is the enfeeblement of the group, as each one waits to be covered by the others but none has the will or the maturity to become not only a receiver but a giver as well. One is not ready to express his double role and, naturally, one is not ready at all to undertake the responsibility of working towards covering the common gaps that are created in everybody by their common needs and difficulties.

The procedures for the passage from the position of the receiver to the position of the person who recycles the soul's energies and powers with others, are procedures that help the next awareness to develop; the fact that everybody is capable of being a giver. The difficulties appearing during a group effort contribute to this and this effort is sometimes inhibited by the members' instability and by their non consolidation in the position of recycling. The problems caused by this instability emphasize the need for the expression of a clearer position of the giver by somebody. This means that it is vital to express the field of consciousness that does not demand to receive something from the others in order to give to them but he simply gives, drawing strength from his very own self. When a person makes this passage of consciousness, when even only one member acknowledges and expresses his inner power, then the group he belongs to automatically acquires a point of reference. It acquires the source of strength personalized in this person, needed by the other members, until they also discover the strength that exists within them and they become autonomous and self-recycled as well.

THE SPIRIT
OF THE GROUP

There are groups the members of which seek a person to become their guiding mind and coordinate their work. They see in him the group's head and they entirely invest in his intervention regarding their problems' settlement both in practice and in the relationships existing among them. Their quest may eventually bring a result and someone may appear who tries to give a proper flow to the group's function. His effort, however, may not always be followed by the expected success; often it does not lead anywhere and it may even cause greater problems to the group's work. Then, everybody resents this situation, they commune among themselves and search to find the cause of their mistake. The responsibility for it is transferred to another person and all together blame the one who undertook the task to help them, but finally led them to new difficulties.

The fault for the errors does not lie in a person; it lies in everybody and the correct stance leads them to success. The members of the group, just like any other human being, have individually reached various levels of consciousness, interacting with each other and composing their group's level of consciousness. This is depicted in every one of their functions and not only in the works they perform, but also in the leader they select. If the synthesis of their individual levels is, for example, the absence of will and action, from which they wish to escape, even though they might believe the opposite, then they unconsciously attract as their leader someone who is also inactive, without any will, unable to release them from this situation. But even if the person they select does not occur to share this attribute and has the will to help them, their resistance inhibits his efforts most of the time. If, though, the common level of the group's consciousness is a different one, such as confidence in themselves, even though not externalized, they select for their leader someone who expresses this and who will help them express it as well.

According to this analysis, we are led to the conclusion that no person, no matter how dynamic his or her presence might be, can help a group express a proper stance if the latter refuses to do so, or if it hasn't realized its hidden abilities. The leader cannot make its members express the group's spirit, power, solidarity, cooperation and love. This conclusion is proved to be right by the examples of the groups whose members always remain in a situation of conflicts and difficulties. They seek new leaders but they do not manage to form a collective spirit and, thus their problems are perpetuated or increased. Nevertheless, there are also exceptions to this rule. There are groups that have substantially changed through a person's positive intervention; he has brought out the spirit of the group and led them to a dynamic expression and function.

To understand the way in which a person may contribute to the collective spirit's formation, we must firstly seek the cause that obstructs this formation. As is already known, a lot of barriers inhibit the development of a group mentality, such as egocentrism, personal problems and reduced interest in the common goals. Behind any causes though, there is a more profound one in which all others find their root.

Behind these causes is hidden ignorance about what "group spirit" really means and how it functions. The same applies for the need to remain in this ignorance, due to fear, insecurity and immaturity. This need comes into conflict with its opposite one, the wish to acquire knowledge and their conflict always causes new difficulties. As long as ignorance prevails, personal egos dominate as well, bringing arrest to the emergence of the group's spirit, or letting it express only in a subfield, via which a respective sub-field of the group's aims is realized.

We are speaking of "group spirit" and by his term we mean the coordinated efforts of some people to perform a common work. In reality, though, the spirit to which we refer is only a very limited expression of the pure Spirit. If we called it "group desire", "group interest", "group emotion", "group mental effort", we would then be using a more accurate term and we would be closer to the truth. Naturally all these are manifestations and expressions of the human spiritual level, but they are not the absolute field of the Spirit. Because Spirit is not confined to some ways of manifestation and it is not only human or only global; it is universal, it is the Spirit of the Monad. Our ignorance of the unlimited field of the Spirit makes us see it only in the part of it that we each time realize, know and express.

Apart from our ignorance about the significance and the breadth of Spirit, the usage of this word to mean its various sub-fields expresses something else as well; and this is the exact opposite of ignorance. It is the proof of the profoundly hidden knowledge existing within us regarding the meaning of the term. It is also an unconscious recognition of the spiritual existence's presence within every one of its projections and within all the subfields of its expression. It is, finally, a way to externalize our great need to realize the Spirit's existence in everything in the physical world, in the world of emotions and in the world of thoughts. The repetition of the word contributes to the consolidation of the notion and to a person's union with his or her spiritual nature. The nature that is never changed no matter how much it is misinterpreted, confined and reversed out of ignorance or denial of the union with it.

People would probably never reach the stage of making an effort to draw out the group spirit if it weren't for some of their common needs. These are what incite them to form groups and pursue the cooperation needed that will help them achieve their common goals. Their pursuits and their visions are analogous to the kind of needs they have. If their need is a material one, then financial security and acquisition of material goods become their vision. If their need is a spiritual one, their vision has to do with a spiritual work, or with their spiritual evolution. Despite the groups' efforts, the realization of their vision is not easily achieved. It may differentiate during the course towards its realization; it may also be confined or even completely lost. Then, the possibility of the group spirit's emergence is also lost and groups fall apart, since they have no reason to exist without sharing a common vision. This does not happen only when the goals of their members are financial and the individual interests may conflict with each other. It may also occur when their goals are spiritual ones, if the element of appropriation intervenes again by members who want to prove that they are the best or that the success of a group is their own personal achievement.

The reasons that encumber the emergence of the group spirit are many but they are all summed up in one: the difficulty man has in seeing spherically the parts of a whole, in composing them, and then referring them to the one, where they belong. It is his need to color the sub-fields of the whole and categorize them into superior and inferior, into individual and group. Colorization and categorization are present everywhere in nature, not to imprison us in some of their aspects, but to form a harmonious aggregate all together. As long as we see only part of this aggregate, it is like seeing nothing at all. It is like standing in front of a painting and looking only at one of its colors or points. This way we cannot see the painting or realize the message the painter wants to convey. At the end we even forget him, its creator. We do the same when we isolate only one manifestation of life, a single individual or an event, forgetting the total it is part of, losing in this way the message conveyed with its presence by the power that made it and generated it.

The one Spirit within everybody and everything can only be expressed by a group, when its existence is acknowledged by all its members. When a spiritual aspect is acknowledged within its goals, no matter what they might be. When within everybody's limited manifestations another spiritual aspect is again acknowledged, no matter what these goals are. When in everybody's confined manifestations – even in the need for appropriation – the unrealized, hidden spiritual essence is acknowledged. When, finally, the spiritual work is acknowledged within a group work no matter the level it expresses, since everything is a level of the Spirit. If such an acknowledgement of the Spirit's presence has been realized, even by only one of the group's members, then the emergence of the real group spirit is very probable. Because, as the broadened level of consciousness of the one interacts with all the others' respective levels, his broadening helps them to become also broadened. This way their evolution is made easier.

From one level of consciousness and on the members of a group know that their leader and guiding mind is not one person. It is the spirit of this person, also being the spirit of the entire group and of every group; not only of the human ones, but also of the groups of the solar systems and galaxies. The Spirit is the only leader of everything. All other leaders are in a state of delusion, since they do not see the spiritual power within themselves and within all the members of their group. For this reason they frequently lose their inner position, they lead the group to failure or to a minimal achievement of its goals. But, even if its goals are reached, success lasts only for some time and then it faces the danger of being lost among life's upheavals. This occurs because these leaders derive their power from a field of consciousness and realization to which they get attached and not from the spirit generating all fields and always remaining within them. The changes in needs, goals and visions leave them without their familiar field that they used as a source of power until then. So, they pass to a position of weakness.

People spiritually evolved, beings consciously united with the spiritual nature, never lose the power that can guide a group. They do not lose it, because they do not see it only within them; they see it and acknowledge it within all the members of the group, within all human beings and within all of their manifestations. They see everywhere the spiritual power that maintains and evolves everybody, even if they are not aware of it. They see the Spirit in everything and in nothing. How is it then possible for their power to be lost, since it is within and beyond all forms? How can they be deprived of something that they had never considered to be their own, because they knew that they are a part of it? Even if they never take the position of the leader of a group they always lead it internally, not as personalities but as conscious spiritual beings, as the Spirit.

Spiritual leadership is magnificent because it is the only one leading to absolute freedom. Whoever accepts it and experiences it within his self becomes free from identification with the fields and the subfields of consciousness, from colorings and categorization. He transcends the bonds of his self and the bonds of the groups he belongs to, diffusing his spirit in every group, the small and the infinite ones, all together forming the one group, the universe, the Monad. He remains on the human level as well, both the individual and the group level, without being subject to these but constantly working for their evolution. He surrenders it with absolute confidence to the Spirit, the guiding mind of all beings and all groups. He does not ask anybody to guide him, because he is united with the one and only guide, the Spirit of the universal world that gives him fulfillment and bliss throughout eternity.

EXISTENCE
AND NONEXISTENCE

A person begins to explore his or her nature by posing the following question to himself: "Who am I? What am I?" In the course one follows in order to find the answer, this question changes many times. Sometimes it is limited to other questions concerning some of a person's aspects, and at other times it broadens out to include one's questions about other people, about the world, about life. Through constant exploration, through experiences and the knowledge one acquires, the initial question begins to be answered on certain levels. One then believes he is on the way to finding the answer that completely covers his question.

Satisfied by what he has already learned, he continues his studies in the awareness of the fact that there are many things he does not know. And then, as a result of the acquired knowledge, the next question emerges within him: "Am I or am I not?" He is overwhelmed, surprised, feeling as if he were in a situation of voidness. All the answers he gave to his previous questions seem arid and insubstantial. What is the meaning of knowing who he is, if he is finally to realize that "he is not at all", that he does not exist? The prospect of such a discovery scares him, and he often refuses to carry on with his research. There are cases though, when his self repeats the same catalytic question so persistently that in the end one is forced to succumb to its will and seek the answer.

The distance between the two questions is huge, that is between the questions of "Who am I?" and "Might I not be?". It is much easier to explore one's nature than to explore the possibility of one's nonexistence, even if attributes that displease one are very often revealed and disappoint one. Comparatively, it is much simpler to cross the personal ego's borders, breaking the barriers of one's own individuality and by extension of all individuals in every other group. Because ıf one is not existent it is self-evident that all others cannot exist either. And if nobody exists, then what is left?

The idea of the self's nonexistence comes into conflict with the need to exist. People want to live to be something, to have something. They want to have a body, a consciousness, a presence. For this reason, they get passionately attached to life even when they are unhappy, ill or abandoned. It is rare for them to reach a point where they want to die, even though they may believe that death does not equal nonexistence, that it only means transition. Even more rarely do they reach the point of accepting that they might be nonexistent and that what they themselves believe of existence is but a fictitious reality.

Due to great attachment to life and existence, the necessary attention to the question "Am I or Am I not?" is not given so that a certain revelation may follow. Many times this question is encountered in such a way that it is considered to be illogical, characterized as a figment of a sick imagination. Most people do not even listen to the inner voice asking them if things exist, but even among those who listen to it, there are very few who wish to know if the question hides any truth at all. All the others directly convince themselves of their existence, since they have a body, they breathe, they feel, and they think. Soon, the question is buried again in the unconscious field from which it had emerged; it escapes memory and is forgotten and lost. In this way a person loses the chance to get to know the profound significance of nonexistence and be united with another range of consciousness, another dimension beyond his already known dimensions.

In spite of all the difficulties in accepting non-existence which are encountered by somebody who wants to search what it is and what it really means, there are some people who want to go on with their exploration. Before proceeding to a deeper study, it is natural to pose some questions to those they consider to be experts in the subjects or to their own selves as well. One of them probably concerns the way the theory about nonexistence is proved. Another one may express their engrossment in the benefit of such a research. And a third may hide the fear that if a person is convinced that he is nonexistent he will cease to have interest in life and will be overwhelmed by sadness or indifference, considering that everything is vain and arid.

These questions are very logical, showing how much a person is attached to his own logic. They indicate his need to analyze, compose and comprehend functioning only through his specific mind, not being able to pass beyond the mental fields he is aware of and be released from them, experiencing real union with notions, with situations, with his deeper self. Nonexistence is not a theory, or some knowledge; it is an experience. If somebody tries to interpret it and analyze it, he automatically gives it form and hypostasis and therefore turns it into existence. Only if he escapes his mind's borders, will he able to experience and become himself what really exists beyond the field of the specific mind.

Wise and enlightened people, who experience non-existence, never describe it. They simply say that whoever passes to it is completely free from the bonds of existence; he does not want anything anymore, thus experiencing fulfillment and bliss. The only thing they teach to those interested in listening to them is that the sole path leading to the situation of nonexistence is non-desire. They also say that the one who does not wish anything for himself loves everything and everybody, and he is united with the whole world, with all of life. And it is this absolute love that connects him with existence and he becomes existent himself. Existent but nonexistent at the same time, without any personal desire but with the only will to express infinite love for existence, which relies on its desire to exist.

Judging from the works and deeds of those proven to have been wise and enlightened, even if we are not able to comprehend the way they function, we will ascertain that the state of nonexistence they experience does not make them indifferent towards life. On the contrary, they are led to absolute interest in it and to love for all of its manifestations. Indifference and apathy is where somebody is led when he wants to be released from everything he does not like, and escape a hard reality that does not cover his countless desires. But if somebody has no desires at all, then he lives every moment without any resistance towards what it brings, since he does not want something else, different than that appearing each time before him. Therefore he remains peaceful, full and self-sufficient among everything and beyond all, always ready to respond to everything those who have not reached his own fulfillment ask him.

The question probably arises: Is it ever possible for a simple, ordinary person to reach such a level of consciousness, to know and experience the simultaneous existence and nonexistence of his self? Is it meaningful to occupy himself with the experiences of the enlightened beings, while his own mind is still in the darkness of ignorance? Everything is possible and everything is meaningful. If one person has been able to become wise, why couldn't this happen to everybody, since wisdom is not anybody's property and since everybody can work in order to reach it? If one has expressed the stance to be redeemed from ignorance and from all the problems it creates, why not believe that the same cannot be expressed by everybody? Our occupation with those who precede us in the path of evolution is meaningful and its meaning is very essential. It encourages us to follow their footsteps; it gives us an example to imitate and empowers our faith in ourselves. All these accelerate the rhythm of the procedures leading to the acknowledgement of our existent and our nonexistent entity.

Saying that we all share the potential to change and evolve is because everything exists within everybody; every idea, every situation and every field of consciousness. Certain moments of revelation come to everybody, making us experience something different from the everyday and the usual. What does the mind do sometimes? Does it not cease to think; doesn't it empty completely from ideas? And isn't it then that we feel like we don't exist, like we are nothing, even if this sensation disappears within a few seconds? Aren't there also times when we feel complete, like nothing is missing and we have no desire? And don't some unexpected realizations come, that our self is a huge embrace that loves everybody? All these things happen to us; they are experiences we all have, but we do not consciously do this. Our inner self does it, our entity, to show us who we really are. That is why this experience is soon lost with only its memory to remain along with the hope that it will come again to give us fulfillment.

What must a person do to be always united with truth, with his self? To exist or not to exist? To love but not to desire? The person himself replies to these answers, the self replies to the self through the voice of his consciousness:

"Do not do anything you imagine that you must do. Do not go after evolution and enlightenment. Do not wish to express love and be released from desire. Do not seek inexistence or existence. Simply consider that you are all these. This is enough! The consideration will lead to the acknowledgement of reality and acknowledgement will bring revelation. And then you will become what you are, what you have always been but you did not know it. You are existence and nonexistence, you are love and non desire, you are all their opposite fields as well, and all of their inter-stages. You are everything, because you are part of Everything, part of the indivisible One."

GOD AND HUMANS

"What is God?" a child asks his parents and an adult asks himself or those whom he believes are able to give him the reply he wants. Parents reply, the self replies, everyone having pored over this subject replies; religion offers a reply as well. The question, though, keeps recurring; at times, from people having previously posed it and, at other times, from others who have suddenly, for the first time, felt the need to learn. Responses repeat themselves, given more analytically or in a more composite way and more broadly, or in a more absolute and catalytic way. Centuries pass, generations succeed one another and people still seek knowledge about God's nature. Man believes in something he comprehends, or he questions what he hears wishing to gather more and more elements in order to become aware of the truth.

The great differences in views expressed by people are the outcome of the research made this far about God's nature. There are those who believe God does not exist, those who firmly believe in His existence, and others who constantly sway between faith and faithlessness. Some people consider God to be impersonal; others see Him only in one person, whereas still others recognize Him in the people of the whole world. To some, God means love, to others, wisdom and to others indifference. Many people call him "Creator" and place Him somewhere outside the perceptible world, whereas others recognize His existence only in the creation, in the universe and in the material forms.

Countless are the opinions on God, sometimes different and opposed to each other and at other times similar or harmonized with each other. The way one uses to communicate and unite with Him depends on the belief he has in one of these opinions. He praises, he prays, he hymns, he gratifies. He can however, do the opposite: demand, get angry or finally be indifferent towards His existence. His idea about God certainly influences his feelings about Him, if He loves Him, or if he is afraid of Him, if he admires, or if he criticizes Him. And according to his emotions he wishes to always feel His presence close to himself or to ignore it and believe that in this way he distances himself from Him.

A person sees God through a human prism. He sees Him with his human qualities which he conveys to Him from himself. One wants him to be present in order to be able to ask Him whatever he or she wants. Nevertheless, what one usually needs is very different from what one really misses; God does not give it to him and for this reason he is often disappointed by what he receives. And as his needs constantly change, his psychological mood also changes as well as his relationship with God. If some new answers are given to him, he may again reject them or, on the contrary, he may get so attached to them that he functions in a sentimental way and becomes fanatic towards the new ideas and views.

A person's usual function towards everything and everybody is an emotional one and the same applies for his or her relationship with God. The human mind comes to give another flow to his function, enriched by specific knowledge. Scientific study, research, and proof interfere until God is presented like a mathematical equation or like a brain without a heart. Emotions and mind bring different currents: on the one hand, arrogance or badly meant humility and on the other hand a mental attitude towards the unknown power that gives form and life to the world. Depending on their view some want to nestle within Him as they were helpless beings. Others want to be directed by him without using their own mind to solve the problems of life.

Denial, fanatic attitudes, passive withdrawal, emotions, accumulation of knowledge. Where do all these lead? Do they lead to union with God or do they lead to doubt and faithlessness finally making us distance ourselves from Him? The reply is given to us by the Saints, the enlightened, the Fathers of the Church, who speak of an entirely different way of humanity's approach to God. They speak of surrendering to the Supreme Will and of trusting His Absolute Love. At the same time, though, they speak of a person's active participation in God's work, of the power, the will and love that he himself must express. They teach absolute interest in every person and love for everything as God exists in everything. Through their actions, they set the example of offering, service and sacrifice for everybody, even for God's deniers, having the faith that only through true love they might also change one day.

God is the One, the Monad, the Absolute. It is This where everybody is born, lives and dies to return again to the source from which their life began. God is everything and nothing; it is existence and nonexistence, the one dimension, every dimension and non-dimension. He is Everything where we exist and from which it is impossible to detach, even if we doubt or deny It. It is beyond everything we can think, comprehend or feel. Thoughts, knowledge and emotions help us because they broaden our consciousness as they overwhelm us by their presence making us realize certain things. As long as we insist on walking through life only through these, we are not able to take the next step. If we do not leave them behind us, if we invest in what they offer us alone, it is like denying the source that has offered them to us, the source that is the Monad, God.

A person walks through life using for his course what he is capable of realizing each time. He is occupied with himself, with others, with humanity, and at the same time he wants to know his divine nature, God's nature. Senses, emotions and knowledge give him whatever he needs in order to keep walking; they give him pleasure and they also give him pain. His desire to learn, to understand, increases; his desire to be redeemed from pain, ignorance and from all ideas that keep on tormenting him increases as well. Until a moment comes when he realizes the vanity of his desires and decides to stop wanting anything, no matter what that might be. Not to want to understand, even not to want to avoid pain and, finally not to insist on knowing with his own mind the infinite and what God is.

When somebody reaches this level, when he has understood what the next step of his course is, then a new procedure begins: whoever completes it is freed from his bonds. He stops his 'I want', his mind finds peace, and he is ready to accept revelation. A revelation that according to those having experienced it, brings fulfillment and peace, it brings the ecstasy that becomes love. None of them describes what he feels though, none can tell what his self is, what it is not, what God overwhelming him is. He knows that his words are incapable of conveying the experience, this personal field. He just lives it and experiences it, whenever it comes, without suffering and seeking it whenever it is lost, and it is as if it does not exist. He does not suffer any more, because he has known the truth, he has known that God's presence is a gift given to the one who stops asking for it. And if someone asks him: "What is God? Where is he?", then he gives a sole reply: "God is everything, he is everywhere, and he is also within you. Love everybody and everything, love yourself as well. Only through love will the truth be revealed to you, because the truth is love and love is God".

EPILOGUE

.

The being's course within the Being. A course from the unconscious to the conscious, from part to the whole, from individual to Monad. The little human being stands up well, as soon as he discovers the existence of his individuality and encounters other people. He becomes their friend, their enemy, their companion or even their opponent. He sees, he comprehends, he is more and more interested in groups, and he slowly begins to form the first small ones.

Years pass, the realizations life brings to people grow along with the groups; they increase, they interact. Procedures about groups' development and life in them continue with many difficulties to gradually form the one group, the group of all humanity. During this course, the human being eventually realizes that he is one with all humanity, that his nature is its nature, its knowledge but also its ignorance as well. When this revelation comes, a new quest begins: the quest of the one and only power existing in the depths of all of his self's aspects alike, in the depths of the aspects not only of every person but of the whole creation as well.

The course of the being within the Being is more consciously made as it advances from the fields of consciousness it has attained to reach union with super-consciousness, with God. New difficulties, doubts and resistances are expressed by its egoistical aspects: by the individual and group needs that inhibit union, hiding the Soul's light, denying the existence of the Spirit. The Being superintends though, It cares for man and directs him throughout his course for finding the truth. And the moment comes when man ceases to resist, ceases to want to exist as something distinct from the Whole and acknowledges the expression of God in his individual existence. He calms down and says to himself:

"Being a minimal particle of the infinite Creation is enough for me. Existing as a human being for as long as my life lasts is enough for me. Having the ability to realize that I am this small, minimal particle of the whole is enough for me. And I admire the power that creates the

world giving life to all beings and maintaining the world in existence.

There are times I would like to face a holy aspect of this Power, an adept, a Saint, a man of superhuman consciousness. I then look at the people around me and think that they all are aspects of the same Power and that they all hide within them the possibility to become Gods and express their divine superhuman self. I also look at myself, and I discover that I have the same holy nature inside me, since I am one of God's beings. And this discovery is a divine gift, offering me peace, faith and fulfillment.

I understand that I do not need anything else anymore. I do not want to learn, evolve and understand. I do not want to have or not to have something, since I have the One that is all within me. I diffuse the fulfillment I experience to all people, and thereby it is like returning the gift I have received to my donator. Because now I know that all things are aspects of Him, parts of God. I also know that what I give is not mine; it is a present that it was given to me in order to know it and then give it to the world as well.

I lead my life in simplicity, united with anything that comes every moment, performing the best way I can my small human work. Everything else, the infinite things, the inconceivable but also the known, I leave entirely to God's Will. And this is enough for me!"

Klairi Lykiardopoulou

Klairi Lykiardopoulou was born in Athens. She went to school at the American College and completed her studies in pedagogy in the United States. She has traveled around the world and has met many different cultures.

Her life changed radically after her acquaintance with Master Dimitris Kakalidis, founder of the "Servers' Society" Spiritual Centre, in 1980. With his guidance, she received his teaching on self-study, on the emergence of the spiritual nature of man and on practicing Spiritual Healing as a way of life. For almost three decades now, she is President of the Society.

She contributed to the structuring of the Servers' Society Healing Section, for which she constantly works by training new healers. Answering unselfishly to the need of the fellow-man, she has met thousands of people who sought help for health, personal, or family problems. On a daily basis she accepts patients who ask for her help through Spiritual Healing, and continues to receive letters of thanks from patients who were healed, either through contact healing or distant healing. Extracts of her book "Spiritual Healing", first published in 1987 in Greece, were presented in sequels in a newspaper of wide circulation, in 1989.

For her literary work she receives commending reviews and is widely appreciated by the country's intellectual world. Extracts of her books have been included in anthologies and literary magazines. Her trilogy about the role of man, woman and the couple was approved by the Hellenic Ministry of Education and Religious Affairs for school libraries. In interviews at the state channel and the radio she has emphasized the need for all people to know and express their true nature.

She has already written 19 books, conveying her personal experiences of her discipleship and developing issues concerning various aspects of life with examples of everyday life, always based on the teaching she has received. An overall presentation of her literary work up until now was held in March 2009, where renowned writers spoke of her offer to the intellect.

Ms Lykiardopoulou continues to work for the task of the Servers' Society, which is the development of human conscience and the dissemination of spirituality.

www.ingramcontent.com/pod-product-compliance
Lightning Source LLC
Chambersburg PA
CBHW070016110426
42741CB00034B/1981